MW01146747

So This Is Me

So this is me...I'm a tad wacky and just shy of crazy.

And I love to create. Whether I'm painting fine art in my studio, drawing my wacky characters on location at shows, sitting at my pottery wheel on my back porch, or writing at my computer, the creative process is liberating beyond words. I am forever exploring new ways to express the energy inside me. But I feel forever blessed to have these gifts and vow to never take them for granted.

I'm 50-something years old and live mere feet from the ocean in a funky little surf town called New Smyrna Beach, Florida. Yes, I know. New Smyrna Beach has been officially declared the "Shark Bite Capital of the World," but the sand sparkles like white crystals and the water is a thousand shades of aqua blue. Waking up every morning to this glorious sight makes my heart tingle. I share that space with my husband, Al, and a goofy Labrador retriever named Lucy. I eat chocolate truffles while I paint—and when they run out, I quit. I drink Perrier sparkling water so often I'm considering taking out stock in the company. I practice yoga, which for some strange reason I think will help compensate for my horrible diet, and I sit on the beach with my toes in the sand every chance I get.

I have five grown children and fourteen grandkids who love me as much as I adore them. I've taught them to dip their French fries in their chocolate shakes, make up any words they want to any tune they like, and to never, ever color inside the lines. (However, they all feel the need to assure their friends that they also have another set of grandparents who are "normal.")

Here are some examples of my work that I have painted with my favorite medium, watercolors.

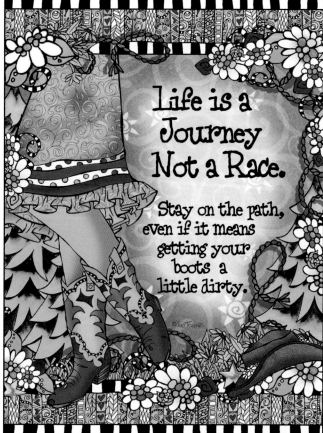

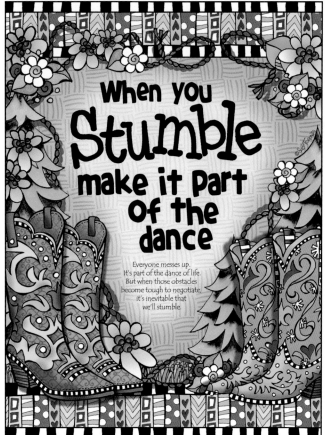

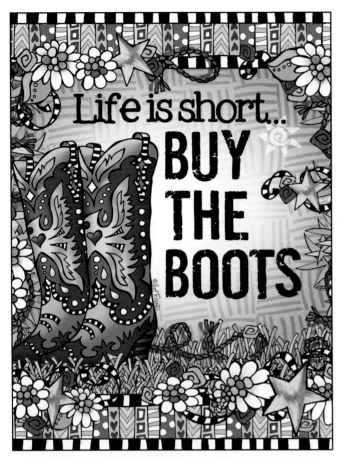

Life is short...
BUY THE BOOTS

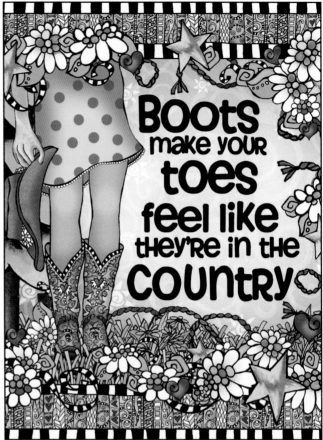

Boots make your toes feel like they're in the COUNTRY

Stop What You're Doing and Start Living

WHEN TAKING THE ROAD LESS TRAVELED IT'S BEST TO WEAR A ROCKIN' HOT PAIR OF BOOTS!

Add the Color...
Feel the Tingle

There's nothing more satisfying than finishing a work of art. It adds excitement and joy to your life. Or to use my favorite tag line, you "Feel the Tingle."

The fact is, not everyone likes to draw, but everybody loves to color. Thus, anyone can experience the joy of participating in creating a piece of art with a coloring book. That's the genius of the medium. It's fun, interesting, and very fulfilling.

It doesn't matter how creative you are, you can learn about color and finish a masterpiece worth displaying. That's the purpose of this introduction—to teach you this skill.

If you already know this stuff, have a ball. If you don't, this information is way worth the effort. It will influence the way you color your entire world, from your home to your clothing to your food. Yes, even how you apply your makeup. And you will become a coloring book guru to boot.

So let's begin.

Color Selection Is Critical

You definitely want that "wow" factor when you're finished. So you need to know which colors do and do not complement each other. Do it right, and it will look like a Picasso.

The most essential tool in color selection is the color wheel, presented to the right. Each color in the wheel is either PRIMARY, SECONDARY, or TERTIARY.

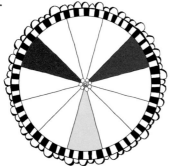

The primary colors are red, yellow, and blue. These are the root colors—they can't be created by mixing other colors. They are the pure foundation of the color wheel. All other colors are some combination of these three.

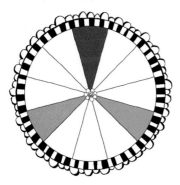

The secondary colors are orange, green, and purple. They are simply an equal mix of two primary colors (red + yellow = orange, yellow + blue = green, and blue + red = purple).

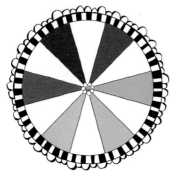

Tertiary colors are created by mixing a primary color with a secondary color. The resulting color is a matter of the percentage of the colors in the mix. There is no end to tertiary colors.

Colors are also categorized as warm or cool. Red, yellow, and orange are warm colors. Green, blue, and purple are cool colors. Selecting warm or cool colors really sets the mood of your piece. Warm colors are bold and exciting, while cool colors are more calm and peaceful.

Things really get interesting when you start playing with variations of a color. You can "tint" a color by adding white to the mix. Or you can "shade" a color by adding black.

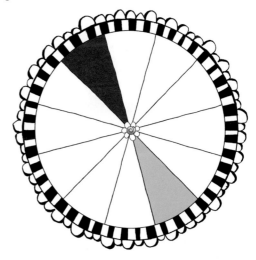

Colors opposite each other on the color wheel are called "complementary" and really pop off the page when they are used adjacent to each other. That's why you see yellow writing on purple backgrounds on billboards all over town. Or vice versa.

My Personal Twist

Since my earliest days as an artist, I have embraced the color yellow. Whether I am painting in my preferred medium of watercolors or dabbling in acrylics, pencils, markers, inks, or crayons, I almost always start with a layer of pale yellow—especially on a piece I want to be on the warm side of the color wheel. This assures that any work of art gets a wash of sunshine, whether the final colors are green, yellow, orange, or red. It really makes the colors pop. Greens get limey, oranges get a tangerine glow, reds get fiery, and yellows get even more electric.

And don't forget to leave open spaces with no color for white. It's easy to want to color every single nook and cranny with one of your fun colors, but leaving enough white is just as important to give your finished piece a lovely balance.

This is how I add a unique touch that is totally me. You should experiment with your own ways to make the art feel uniquely you! You might do this with your color choices or by adding patterns and flourishes to the art. Have fun playing around!

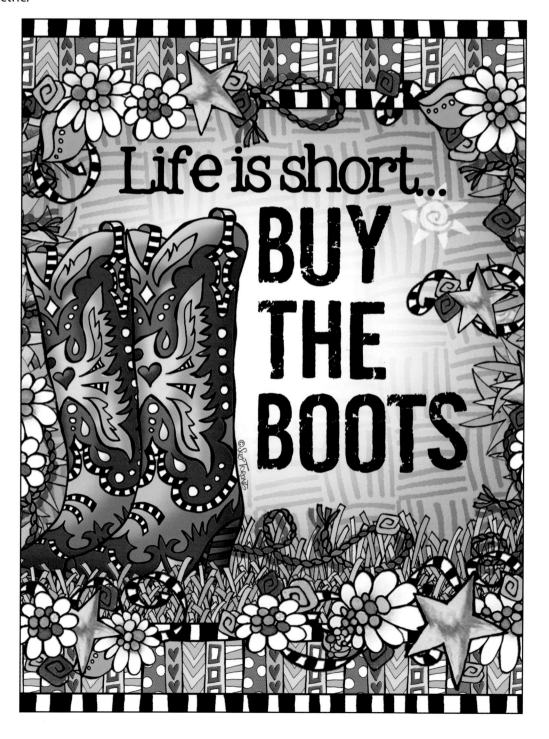

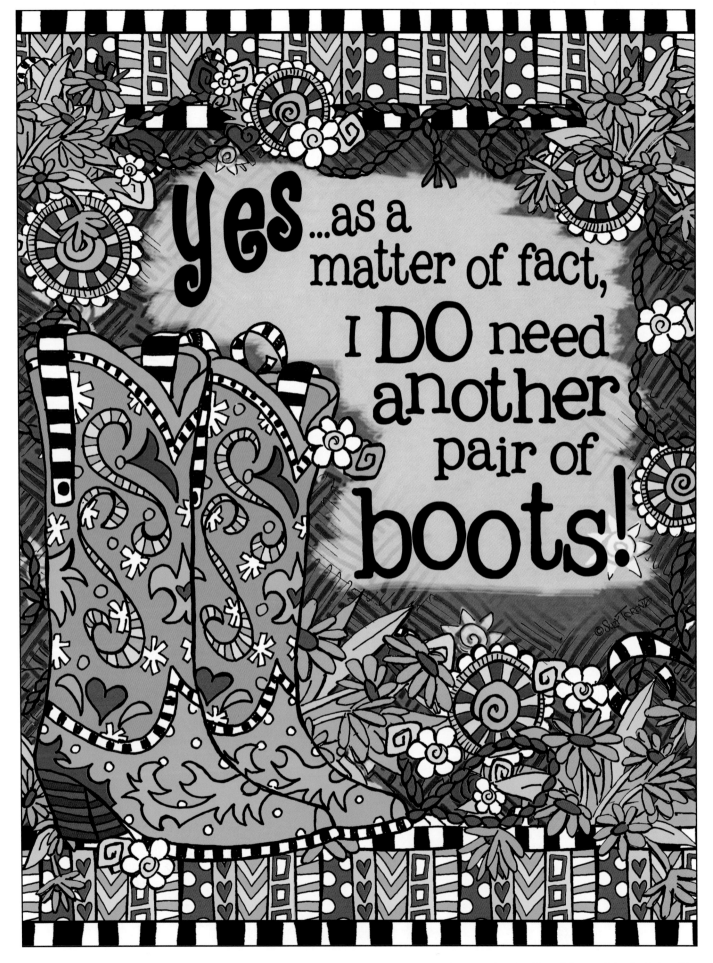

yes ...as a matter of fact, I DO need another pair of boots!

Another Pair of Boots, Color by Robert Thimm

©Suzy Toronto • suzytoronto.com • From *Tingle Boots Coloring Book* ©Design Originals, www.D-Originals.com

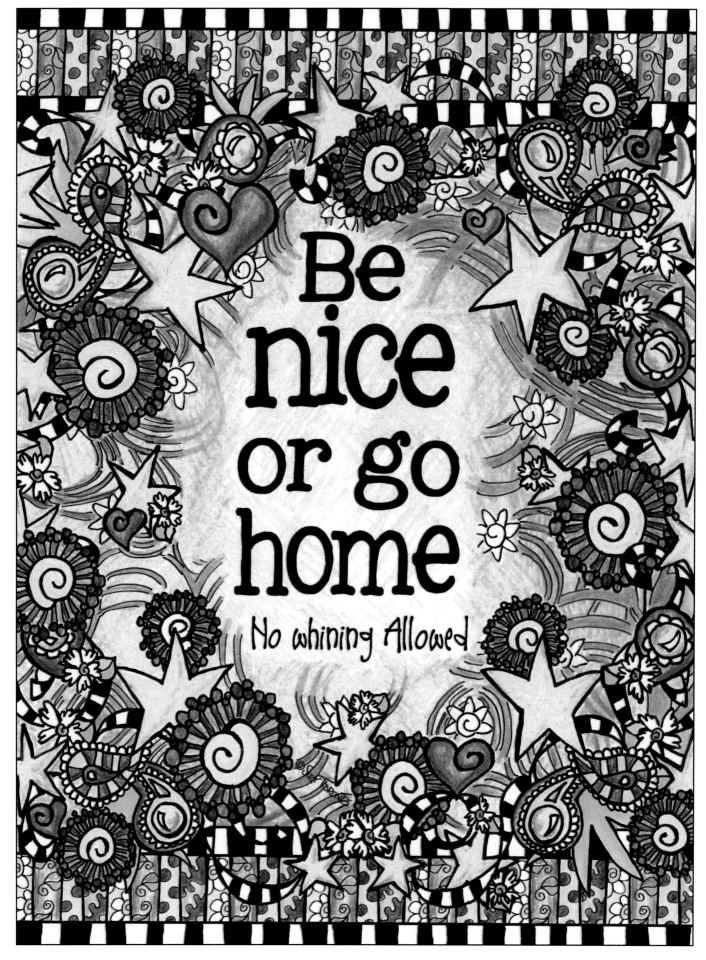

Be nice or go home

No whining Allowed

Be Nice, Color by Robert Thimm

©Suzy Toronto • suzytoronto.com • From *Tingle Boots Coloring Book* ©Design Originals, www.D-Originals.com

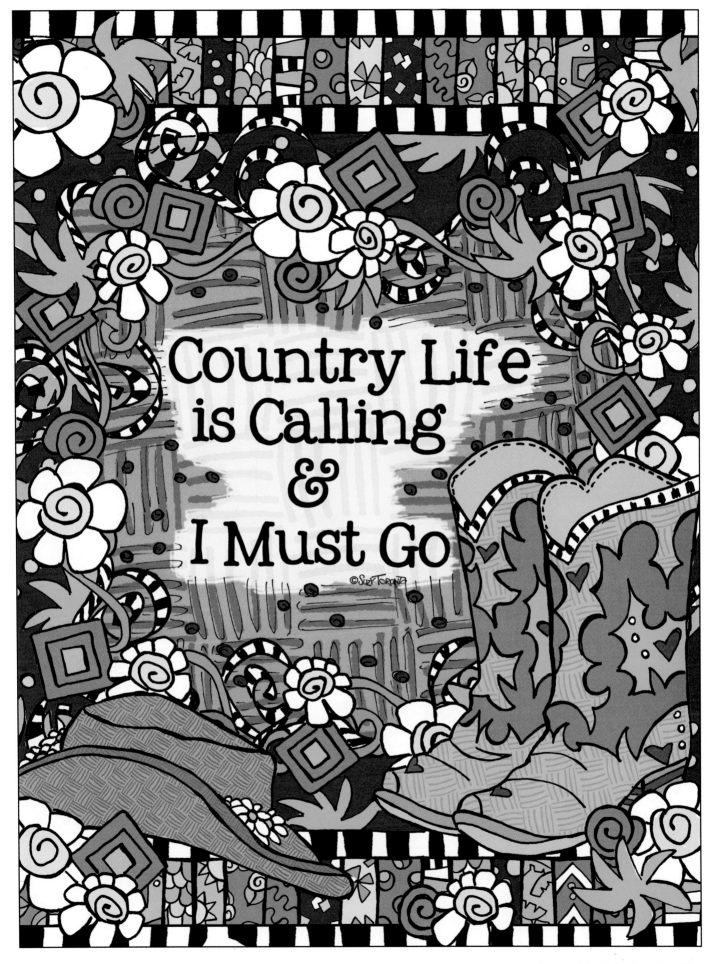

Country Life, Color by Robert Thimm

©Suzy Toronto • suzytoronto.com • From *Tingle Boots Coloring Book* ©Design Originals, www.D-Originals.com

Dream Big...
If That Doesn't Work
Dream Bigger

Have you ever dreamed up a whiz-bang idea,
only to see someone else living your dream
three months later... even selling your idea like hotcakes?
Yeah... me too. Well, the next time it happens,
jump on it! But not just with a little hop.
Plunge on top of it with everything you've got.
Kick it into the stratosphere and make it reality.
Dream really big. If that doesn't work, dream even bigger.
Remember, all great things started as a crazy,
wild idea in somebody's head.
Why not yours?.

©Suzy Toronto

Dream Big, Color by Robert Thimm

©Suzy Toronto • suzytoronto.com • From *Tingle Boots Coloring Book* ©Design Originals, www.D-Originals.com

I'll always choose **Boots Over Heels**

Boots Over Heels, Color by Robert Thimm

©Suzy Toronto • suzytoronto.com • From *Tingle Boots Coloring Book* ©Design Originals, www.D-Originals.com

Wanted: No Regrets (Tingle Boots), Color by Robert Thimm

©Suzy Toronto • suzytoronto.com • From *Tingle Boots Coloring Book* ©Design Originals, www.D-Originals.com

Boots, Class & a Little Sass!
(That's what country girls are made of.)

Country Girls, Color by Robert Thimm

©Suzy Toronto • suzytoronto.com • From *Tingle Boots Coloring Book* ©Design Originals, www.D-Originals.com

Be Brave Enough to be Authentic

I dare you to strip yourself down
to the real you, and be authentic.
Be willing to sacrifice who you are
for who you could become.
Imagine the freedom of going through your day
being unapologetically yourself, marching to
your very own beat, while letting go of the baggage
you thought was necessary to your life.
Embrace the idea that the only person you are destined
to become is the person you truly are inside. Be the architect
of your own destiny. As you embrace your authentic self,
your confidence and self-worth will soar.
You will have the courage to stand a little taller
and reach a little further than ever before.
And your example will encourage others
to do the same. Go ahead. Give it a try!

Be Authentic (Tingle Boots), Color by Robert Thimm

©Suzy Toronto • suzytoronto.com • From *Tingle Boots Coloring Book* ©Design Originals, www.D-Originals.com

Some of the best cowboys... ...are not boys.

©Suzy Toronto

Some of the Best Cowboys Are Not Boys, Color by Robert Thimm

©Suzy Toronto • suzytoronto.com • From *Tingle Boots Coloring Book* ©Design Originals, www.D-Originals.com

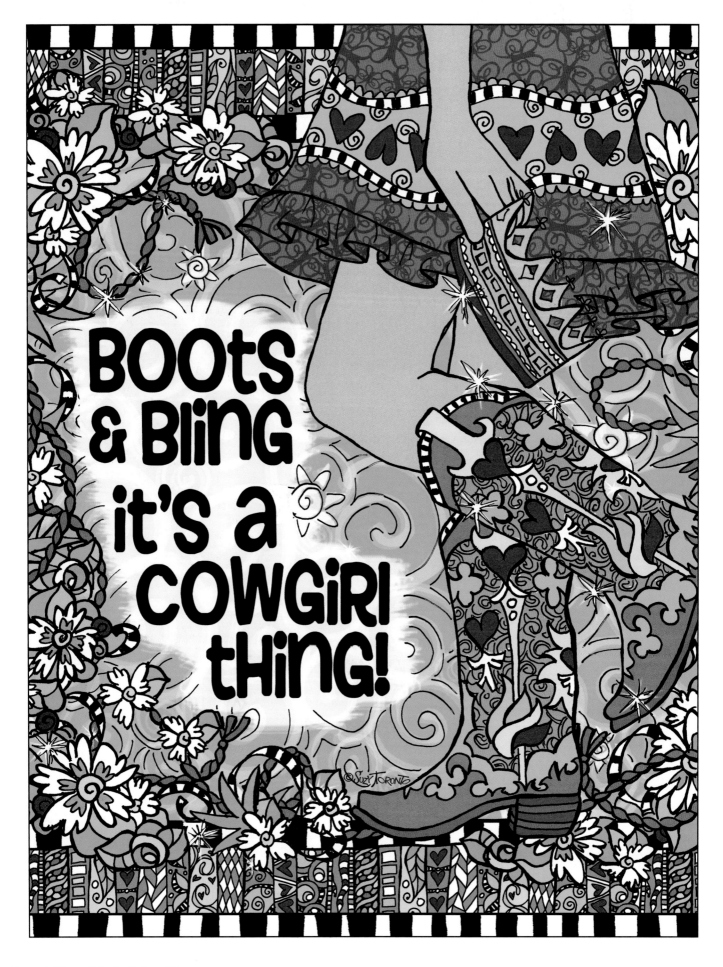

Boots & Bling, Color by Robert Thimm

©Suzy Toronto • suzytoronto.com • From *Tingle Boots Coloring Book* ©Design Originals, www.D-Originals.com

Boots & Bling it's a COWGiRl tHiNG!

©Suzy Toronto • suzytoronto.com • From *Tingle Boots Coloring Book* ©Design Originals, www.D-Originals.com

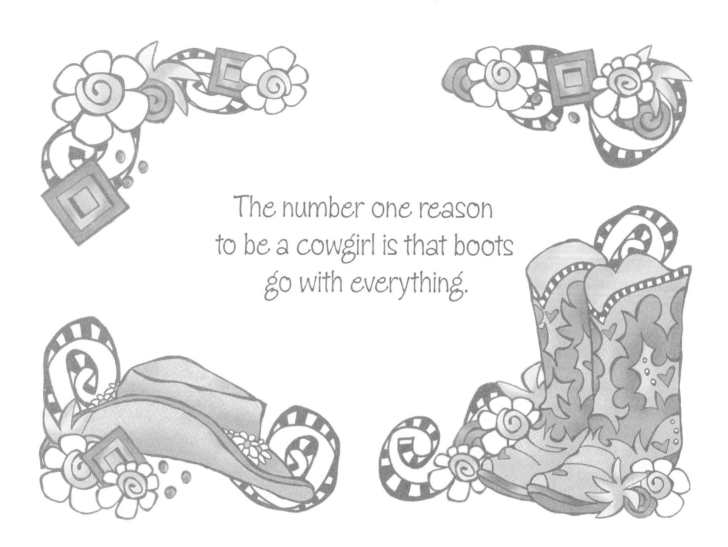

The number one reason
to be a cowgirl is that boots
go with everything.

Boots & Bling (Tingle Boots)

©Suzy Toronto • suzytoronto.com • From *Tingle Boots Coloring Book* ©Design Originals, www.D-Originals.com

"Boot Love" is true love.

Buy the Boots (Tingle Boots)

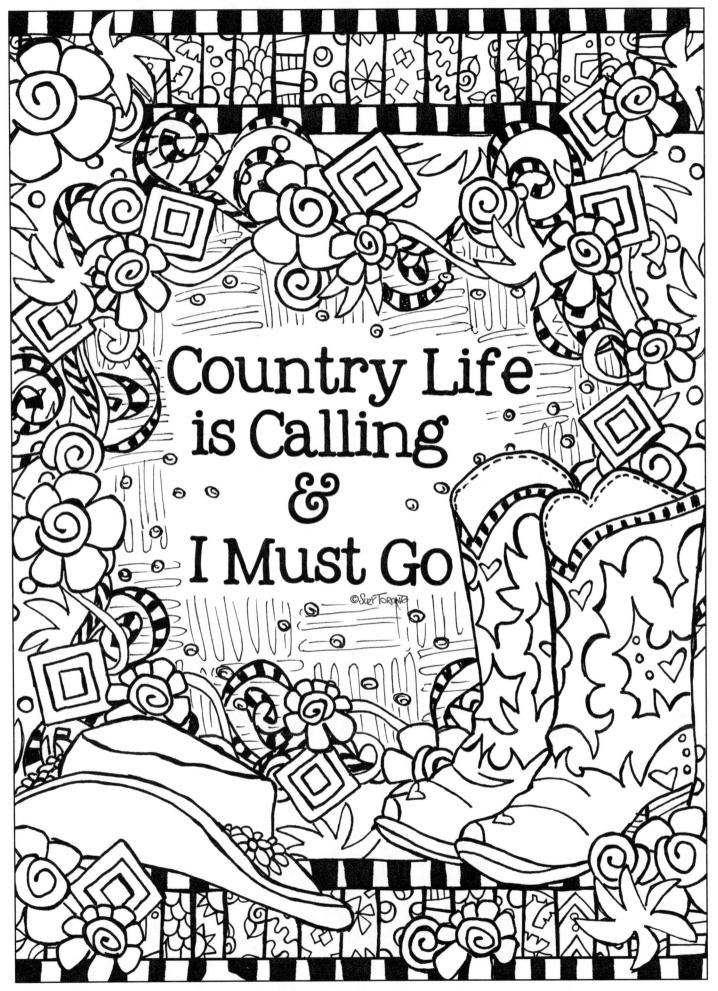

©Suzy Toronto • suzytoronto.com • From *Tingle Boots Coloring Book* ©Design Originals, www.D-Originals.com

Life is better in boots.

Be Brave Enough to be Authentic

I dare you to strip yourself down
to the real you, and be authentic.
Be willing to sacrifice who you are
for who you could become.
Imagine the freedom of going through your day
being unapologetically yourself, marching to
your very own beat, while letting go of the baggage
you thought was necessary to your life.
Embrace the idea that the only person you are destined
to become is the person you truly are inside. Be the architect
of your own destiny. As you embrace your authentic self,
your confidence and self-worth will soar.
You will have the courage to stand a little taller
and reach a little further than ever before.
And your example will encourage others
to do the same. Go ahead. Give it a try!

©Suzy Toronto • suzytoronto.com • From *Tingle Boots Coloring Book* ©Design Originals, www.D-Originals.com

I will never apologize
for being me.

Be Authentic (Tingle Boots)

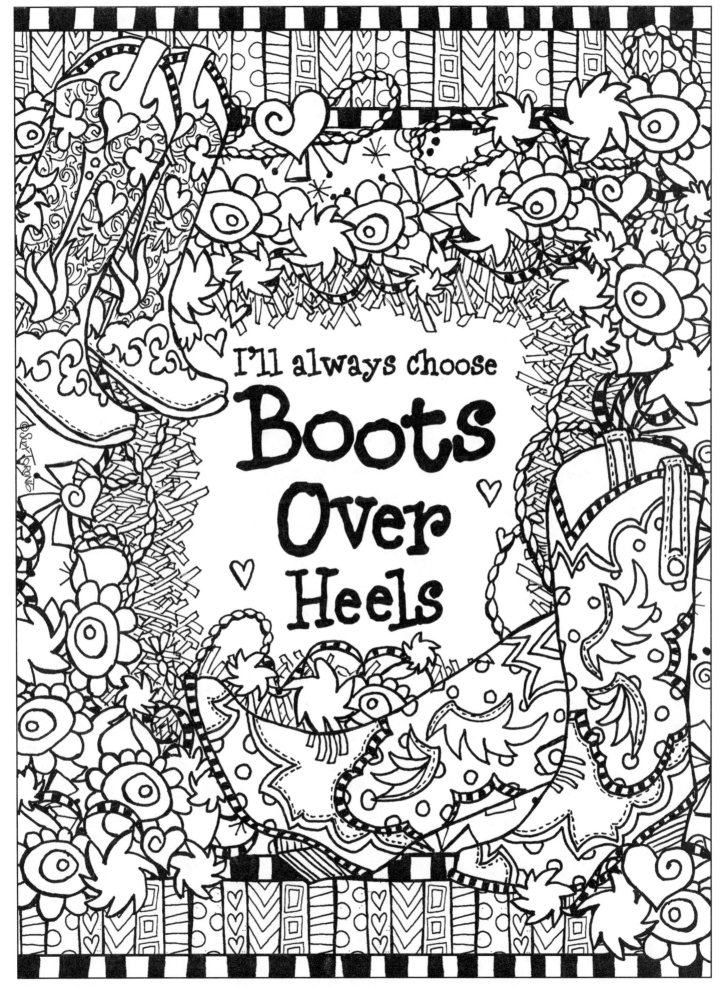

I'll always choose Boots Over Heels

©Suzy Toronto • suzytoronto.com • From *Tingle Boots Coloring Book* ©Design Originals, www.D-Originals.com

I seem to have a problem with
always needing a new pair of boots!

Boots Over Heels

Don't let anyone dull your sparkle

©Suzy Toronto

©Suzy Toronto • suzytoronto.com • From *Tingle Boots Coloring Book* ©Design Originals, www.D-Originals.com

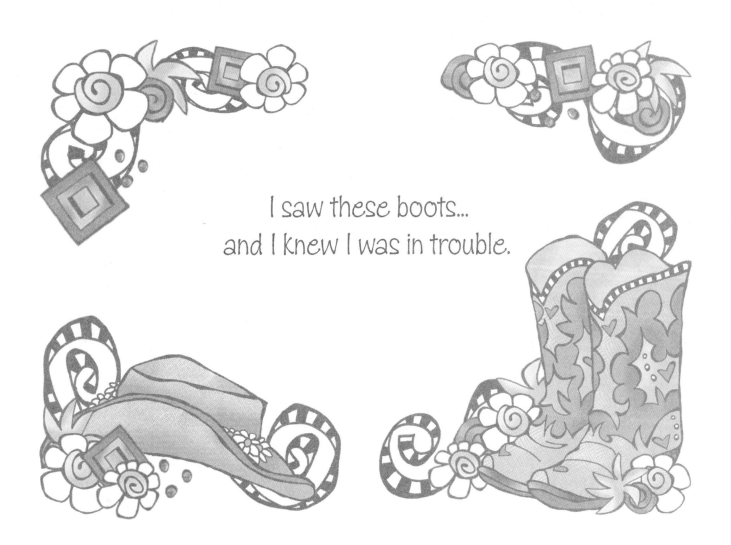

I saw these boots...
and I knew I was in trouble.

_____

_____

_____

_____

_____

_____

_____

_____

Don't Let Anyone Dull Your Sparkle (Tingle Boots)

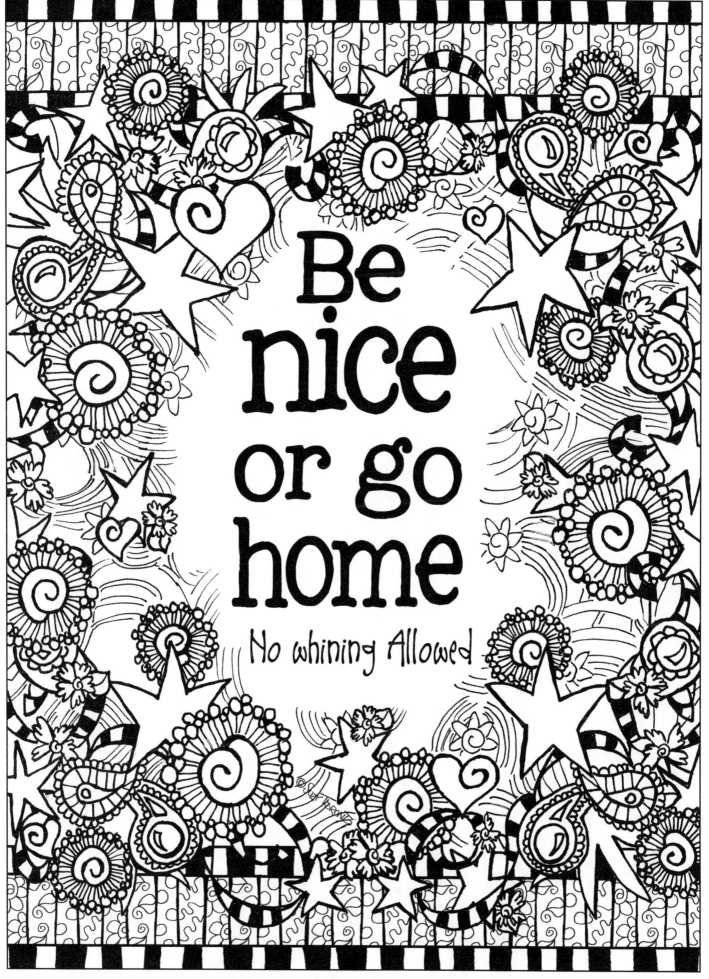

©Suzy Toronto • suzytoronto.com • From *Tingle Boots Coloring Book* ©Design Originals, www.D-Originals.com

Here's to being the best
cowgirl you can be.

Give a girl the right pair of boots & she can rule the world

©Suzy Toronto

©Suzy Toronto • suzytoronto.com • From *Tingle Boots Coloring Book* ©Design Originals, www.D-Originals.com

All things are possible with coffee and cowboy boots.

Some of the best cowboys... ...are not boys.

©Suzy Toronto

©Suzy Toronto • suzytoronto.com • From *Tingle Boots Coloring Book* ©Design Originals, www.D-Originals.com

It's not easy being a cowgirl,
but if the boot fits...

Some of the Best Cowboys Are Not Boys

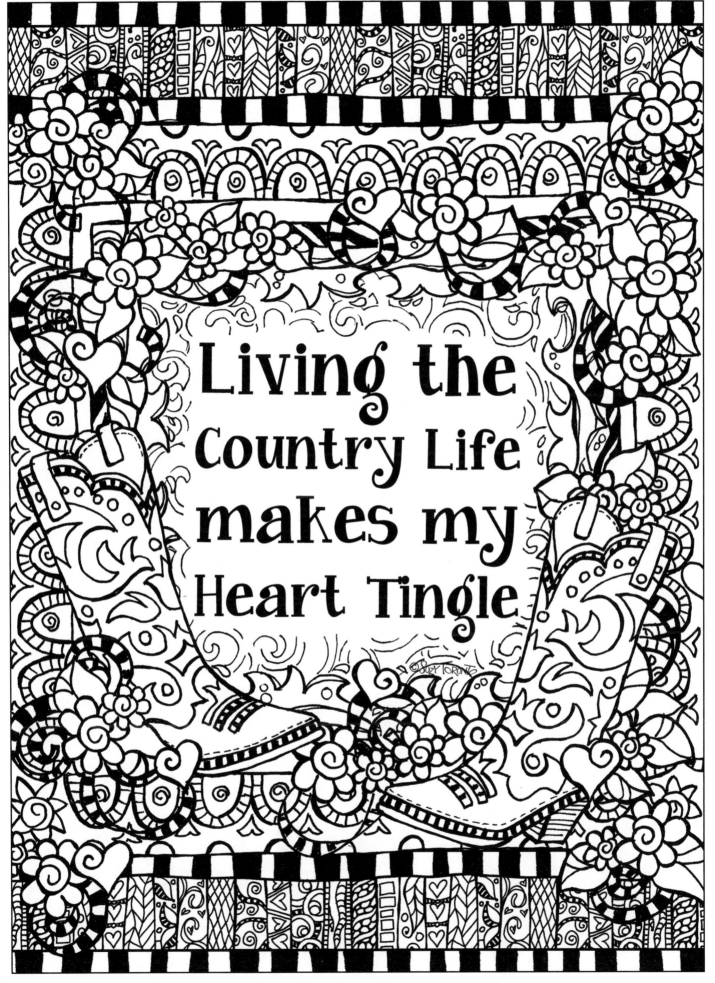

Living the Country Life makes my Heart Tingle

©Suzy Toronto • suzytoronto.com • From *Tingle Boots Coloring Book* ©Design Originals, www.D-Originals.com

It costs you nothing to dream of
a country life and everything not to.

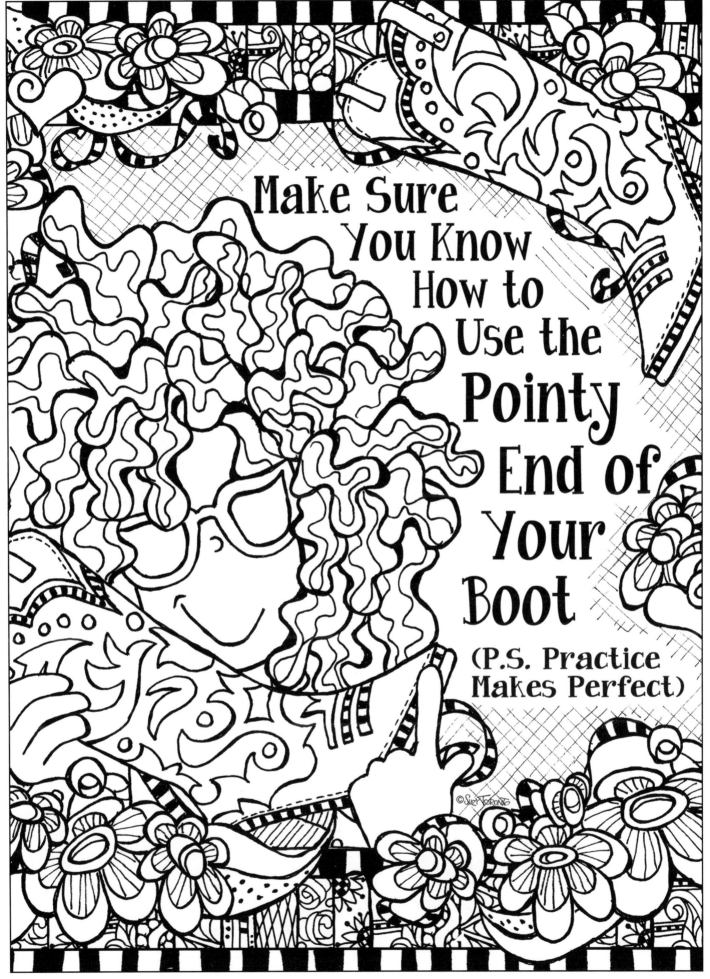

Make Sure You Know How to Use the Pointy End of Your Boot

(P.S. Practice Makes Perfect)

©Suzy Toronto • suzytoronto.com • From *Tingle Boots Coloring Book* ©Design Originals, www.D-Originals.com

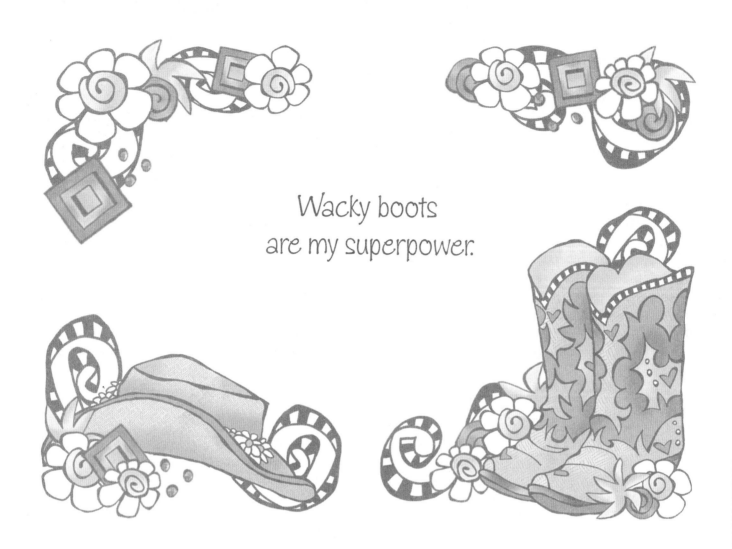

Wacky boots
are my superpower.

The Pointy End (Tingle Boots)

©Suzy Toronto • suzytoronto.com • From *Tingle Boots Coloring Book* ©Design Originals, www.D-Originals.com

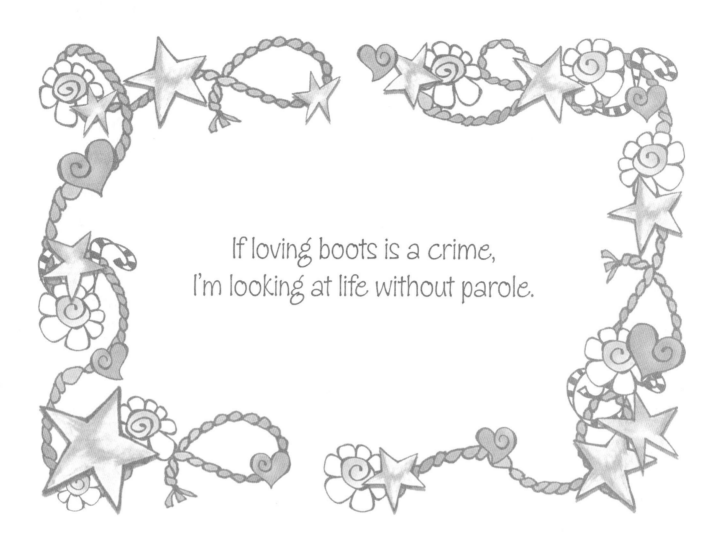

If loving boots is a crime,
I'm looking at life without parole.

Too Many Shoes (Tingle Boots)

It's Time to Get Your Life In Gear

No one wants to live a life of
"would've, should've, could've"…
forever looking back,
second-guessing every decision,
and fretting over what might have been.
Yet it's funny how we can cling to the past,
thinking that we can maybe find a "do over"
button and create a whole different ending.

Well, I have a news flash for you. The past is over!
Nothing you do will ever change that so let it go.
You can start this very moment by honoring
your individual worth and accepting
responsibility for your choices.
   Kick into gear and release the old, embrace the new.
Make today, right here and right now, your focus.
Now is the time for you to live your life
like you really mean it and proceed to evolve into
the magnificent free spirit you always intended to be.

©Suzy Toronto • suzytoronto.com • From *Tingle Boots Coloring Book* ©Design Originals, www.D-Originals.com

All you need is love...
and a new pair of boots.

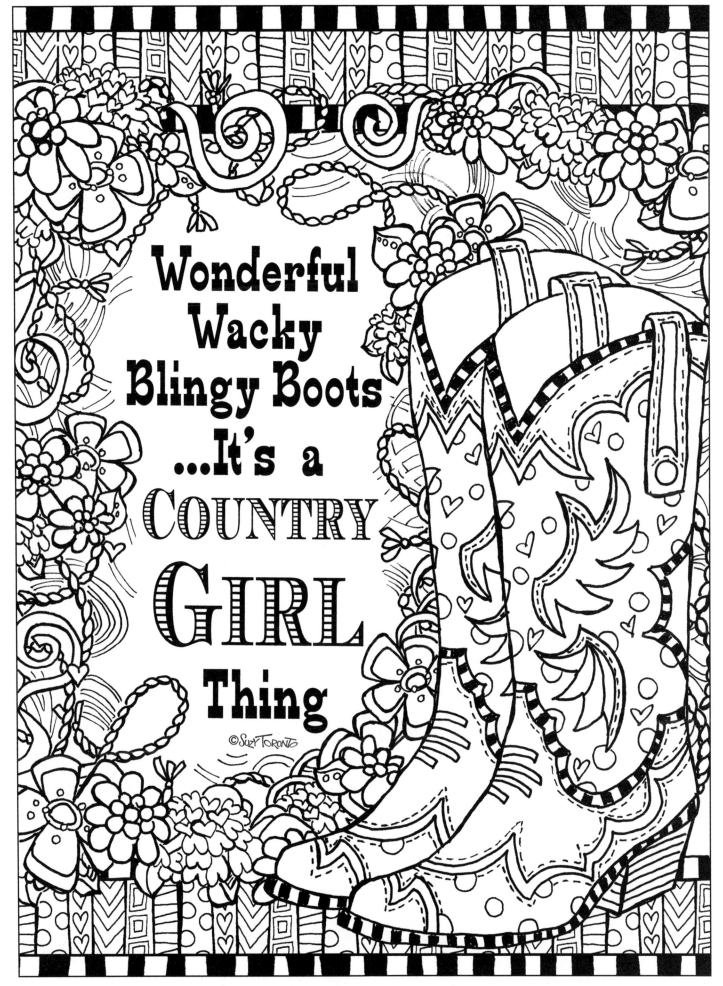

Wonderful Wacky Blingy Boots ...It's a COUNTRY GIRL Thing

©Suzy Toronto

©Suzy Toronto • suzytoronto.com • From *Tingle Boots Coloring Book* ©Design Originals, www.D-Originals.com

Some girls like the finer things in life
but not me...I just want a
wacky pair of colorful boots.

©Suzy Toronto • suzytoronto.com • From *Tingle Boots Coloring Book* ©Design Originals, www.D-Originals.com

When it rains on your parade,
just pull on some really cute boots.

_____

_____

_____

_____

_____

_____

_____

_____

Wanted: No Regrets (Tingle Boots)

Kick Off Your Boots...

Feel the Tingle of Just Being Home

There are few places on earth
that can rival being home.
Sure, there are places to visit with rugged,
majestic mountains or tropical, pounding surf
that have the power to positively
take our breath away.
Yet when the visit is over, the bottom line
is that there is simply no place like home.

©Suzy Toronto

©Suzy Toronto • suzytoronto.com • From *Tingle Boots Coloring Book* ©Design Originals, www.D-Originals.com

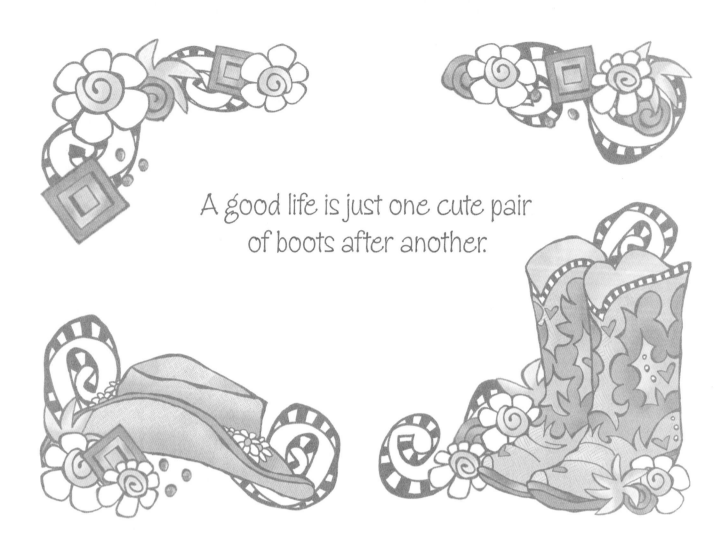

A good life is just one cute pair
of boots after another.

Stop calling me a
TOMBOY
You're just mad
because I'm
ROCKIN'
this pair of
BOOTS

©Suzy Toronto • suzytoronto.com • From *Tingle Boots Coloring Book* ©Design Originals, www.D-Originals.com

Good boots aren't cheap
and cheap boots aren't good.

Wonderful Wacky Words To Make Your Heart Tingle

Life is too short to wear pantyhose ◎ If you want rainbows, you gotta have rain ◎ Don't play life safe; make waves ◎ Life is short, buy the boots ◎ Enthusiasm is contagious ◎ Life is all about how you handle plan B...in the end, it's the true test of character ◎ Art does not have to match your sofa, your hair color... or your boots ◎ Play with wild abandon ◎ Happiness is always an inside job ◎ When life gets crazy, do something normal... and if life gets too normal, do something crazy ◎ When life gets stormy, pull on your boots and go out looking for puddles to play in ◎ Dream with your eyes wide open ◎ And the most important thing to know... age is nothing but a state of mind. ◎ So pick an age you like, and stick to it!

©Suzy Toronto • suzytoronto.com • From *Tingle Boots Coloring Book* ©Design Originals, www.D-Originals.com

"I already own enough boots,"
said no one, ever.

Don't be Calm & Carry On... Pull On Your Boots & Start Kickin'

©Suzy Toronto

©Suzy Toronto • suzytoronto.com • From *Tingle Boots Coloring Book* ©Design Originals, www.D-Originals.com

It's a whole lot easier
to be crazy brave
in a hot pair of boots.

Forget Glass Slippers...

This Princess Wears Boots

©Suzy Toronto

©Suzy Toronto • suzytoronto.com • From *Tingle Boots Coloring Book* ©Design Originals, www.D-Originals.com

I am helplessly, hopelessly
addicted to boots.

chase
your dreams
in the cutest
pair of boots
you own

As children, we were invincible.
We could do anything we dreamed up!
The world was our playground, and there was
no end to the possibilities we could kick up.
As we grew older, that youthful spirit faded,
and we began to question our own talents and abilities.

But now, if you look deep inside your heart
(buried under years of growing pains!),
you can still find that unbridled, childlike conviction.
It's there and it's real, it fans the flames
of dreams, creativity, and imagination.
So release your inner child and believe in yourself again.
There's more inside you than
you ever dreamed possible!

©Suzy Toronto

©Suzy Toronto • suzytoronto.com • From *Tingle Boots Coloring Book* ©Design Originals, www.D-Originals.com

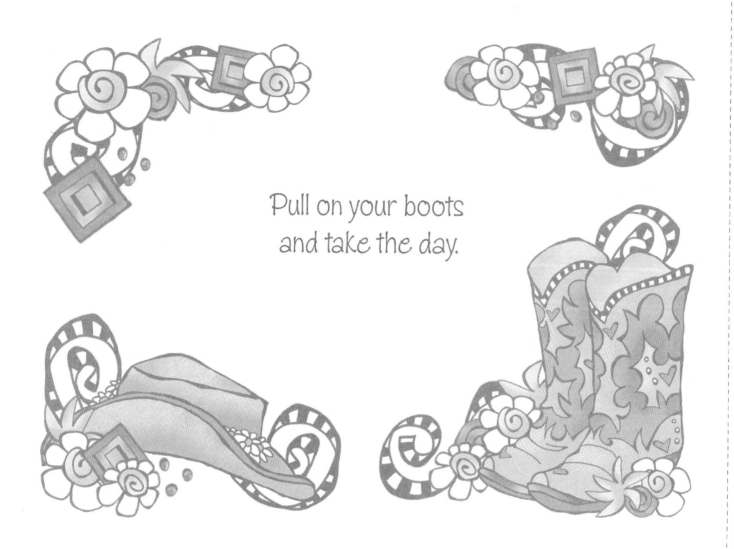

Pull on your boots
and take the day.

Boots make your toes feel like they're in the country

©Suzy Toronto • suzytoronto.com • From *Tingle Boots Coloring Book* ©Design Originals, www.D-Originals.com

I'd rather be lost in the country
than found in the city.

Country Boots (Tingle Boots)

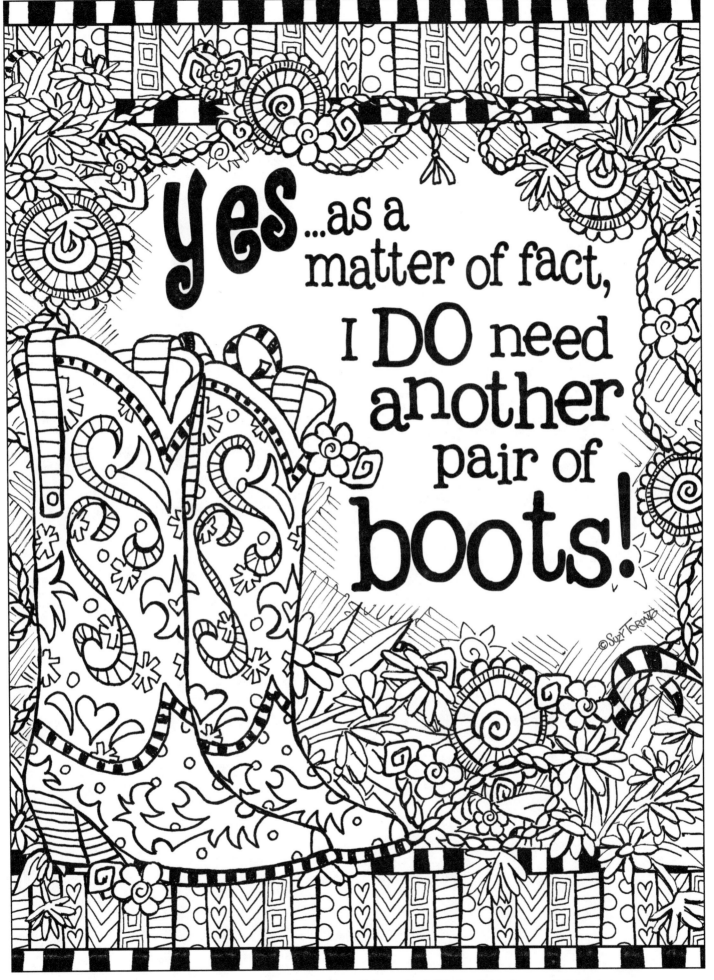

yes...as a matter of fact, I DO need another pair of boots!

©Suzy Toronto • suzytoronto.com • From *Tingle Boots Coloring Book* ©Design Originals, www.D-Originals.com

If I can't wear my boots,
I ain't going.

Another Pair of Boots

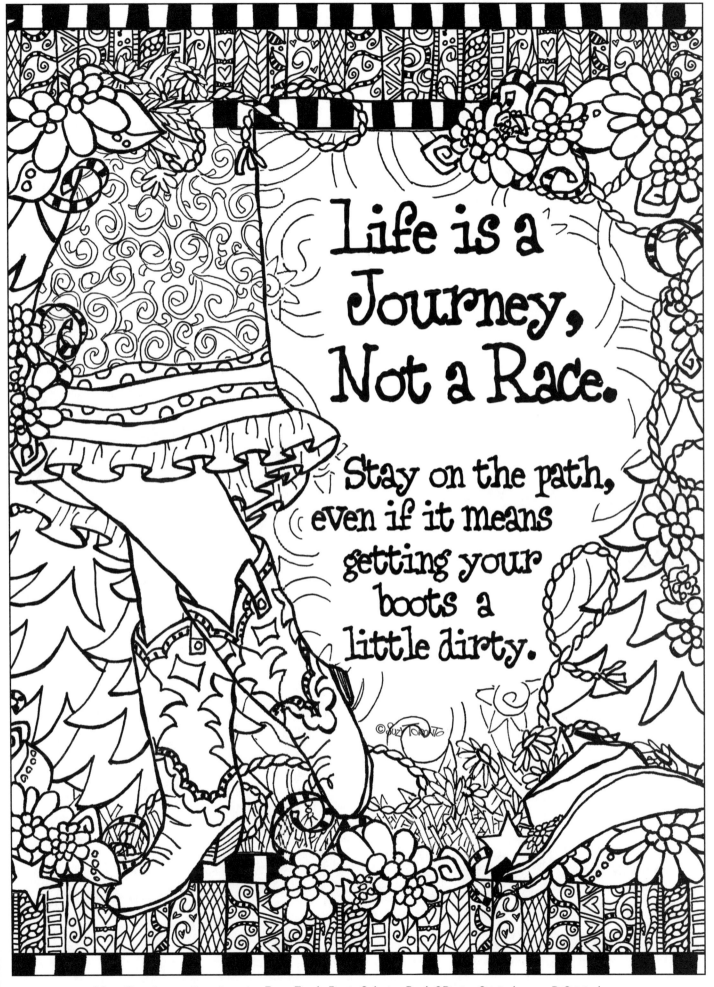

Life is a Journey, Not a Race.

Stay on the path, even if it means getting your boots a little dirty.

©Suzy Toronto

©Suzy Toronto • suzytoronto.com • From *Tingle Boots Coloring Book* ©Design Originals, www.D-Originals.com

I have no idea where I'm going
in this pair of boots, but I
promise it won't be boring.

When you **Stumble** make it part of the dance

Everyone messes up.
It's part of the dance of life.
But when those obstacles
become tough to negotiate,
it's inevitable that
we'll stumble.

©Suzy Toronto • suzytoronto.com • From *Tingle Boots Coloring Book* ©Design Originals, www.D-Originals.com

On the outside, everything
is fine. But deep down inside
my boot, my sock is slipping off.

When You Stumble (Tingle Boots)

Dream Big...
If That Doesn't Work
Dream Bigger

Have you ever dreamed up a whiz-bang idea,
only to see someone else living your dream
three months later... even selling your idea like hotcakes?
Yeah... me too. Well, the next time it happens,
jump on it! But not just with a little hop.
Plunge on top of it with everything you've got.
Kick it into the stratosphere and make it reality.
Dream really big. If that doesn't work, dream even bigger.
Remember, all great things started as a crazy,
wild idea in somebody's head.
Why not yours?.

©Suzy Toronto

©Suzy Toronto • suzytoronto.com • From *Tingle Boots Coloring Book* ©Design Originals, www.D-Originals.com

Be brave, be strong,
and wear wacky boots.

Dream Big

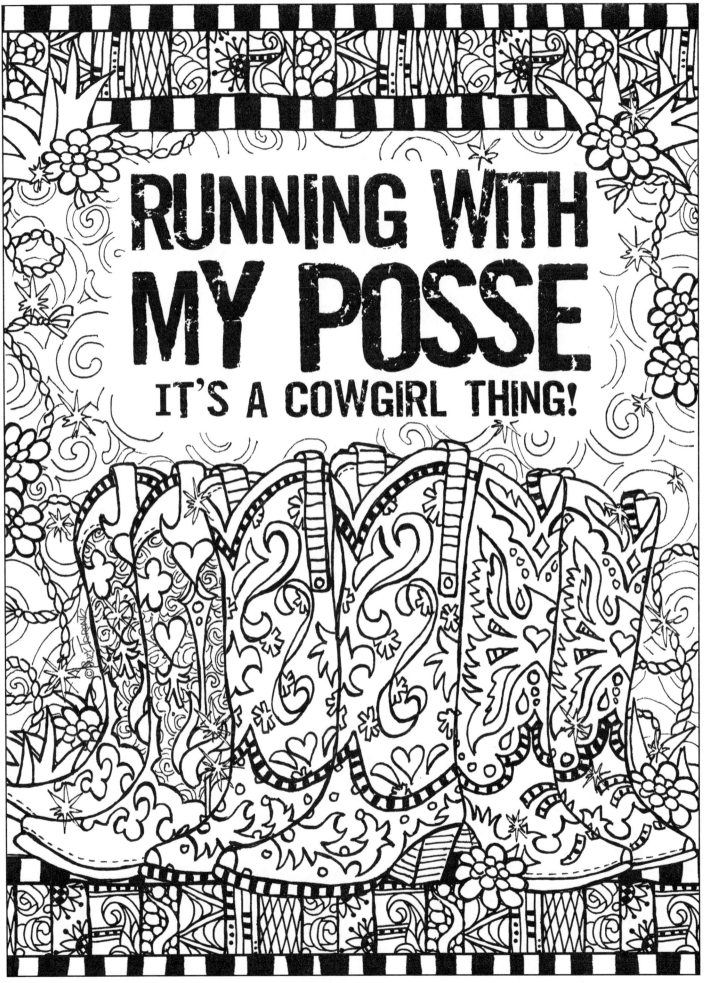

©Suzy Toronto • suzytoronto.com • From *Tingle Boots Coloring Book* ©Design Originals, www.D-Originals.com

The best way to start your day is to pull
on a pair of wacky cowgirl boots.

I am Aware that I am Rare

©Suzy Toronto • suzytoronto.com • From *Tingle Boots Coloring Book* ©Design Originals, www.D-Originals.com

I don't always wear
cowgirl boots, but when I do,
I feel like I rule the world.

I Am Rare (Tingle Boots)

WHEN TAKING THE ROAD LESS TRAVELED, IT'S BEST TO WEAR A **ROCKIN' HOT PAIR OF BOOTS!**

©Suzy Toronto

©Suzy Toronto • suzytoronto.com • From *Tingle Boots Coloring Book* ©Design Originals, www.D-Originals.com

Hot boots take
you good places.

Road Less Traveled (Tingle Boots)

Kindness Never Goes Out of Style

Life is never going to be perfect.
Conflicts are bound to arise and challenges will inevitably come.
A lot of it is simply out of our control. But the only thing
we can control is our attitude and how we deal with it.
We can choose to be whiney, hard-headed and selfish,
or we can choose to be kind, considerate and understanding.

Whenever you can, choose the latter.
When challenges arise, choose to take a deep breath,
try to see the other point of view,
and resolve things with civility.
Strive to be kind...especially when it isn't easy
because you will never regret
being too kind.

©Suzy Toronto

©Suzy Toronto • suzytoronto.com • From *Tingle Boots Coloring Book* ©Design Originals, www.D-Originals.com

Keep your soul clean
and your boots dirty.

Stop What You're Doing and Start Living

©Suzy Toronto • suzytoronto.com • From *Tingle Boots Coloring Book* ©Design Originals, www.D-Originals.com

Boots make my heart tingle
and my spirit soar.

_____
_____
_____
_____
_____
_____
_____
_____

Start Living (Tingle Boots)

Boots, Class & a Little Sass!

(That's what country girls are made of.)

©Suzy Toronto • suzytoronto.com • From *Tingle Boots Coloring Book* ©Design Originals, www.D-Originals.com

I'm a jeans-and-boots kind of gal.